Dedicated to the memory of Christie Jean Caldwell

The Plaza
KANSAS CITY'S WORLD-FAMOUS SHOPPING DISTRICT

David S. Hudson, Editor
Bob Barrett, Principal Color Photography
Gerard L. Eisterhold, Design
Dory DeAngelo, Historical Text
Robert Eisele, Editorial Associate
Roger McDougle, Editorial Associate

Harrow Books
Prairie Village, Kansas

The Plaza/Kansas City's World-Famous Shopping District

First Printing September, 1989

ISBN Number: 0-916455-04-1

Library of Congress Catalogue Card Number: 89-085896

The Plaza

KANSAS CITY'S WORLD-FAMOUS SHOPPING DISTRICT

A Brief History of the Country Club Plaza

By Dory DeAngelo

The Land

The land on which the Country Club Plaza is built has attracted visitors for centuries. The shoppers and tourists who come to the Plaza today walk in the footsteps of many who have come before. Indians, fur trappers, Mormons, Santa Fe traders, and soldiers of the Confederate and Union armies have all crossed this land nestled in the Brush Creek Valley. At the dawn of the 20th Century the valley attracted the attention of Jesse Clyde Nichols. He would change the face of it forever.

For centuries Indians traveled the Missouri River to hunt in the forest that would become Kansas City. Just west of the city is the confluence of two rivers. The Missouri, coming from its origin in Montana, turns eastward streaming toward the Mississippi. It blends with the Kaw River as that river travels east connecting with creeks and rivers in its journey from Colorado. Using these waterways, Indians came from all directions seeking game in the grasslands and forests that stretched out from the rivers' banks.

Some of these Indians stayed long enough to establish villages. The Kanza Indians (from which Kansas City takes its name) had villages on the Little Blue River downstream from Brush Creek. The creek was a watering hole for small animals and thus the Indians could easily hunt there. The Indians used an ancient trail to travel back and forth from the Missouri River. Sauks, Iowas, and Osages tramped south through the forest, up a ravine at what is now Chestnut and Independence Avenue and, crossing Brush Creek at about Troost, continued through southern Missouri to Indian settlements on the Osage River.

Trade with the Indians and fur trappers helped establish settlements at Kansas City. The earliest known fur trapper in the area was Daniel Morgan Boone, son of the famous frontiersman Daniel Boone. He came in the late 18th Century to trap beaver along Brush Creek and began farming south of Westport.

Other fur trappers followed. They sent their animal pelts to St. Louis by way of the Missouri River. The demand for fur hats and coats on the East Coast and the abundance of trappers ready to trade enticed the Chouteau family of the St. Louis-based American Fur Company to establish a trading station near the joining of the two rivers. In 1821, Francois Chouteau brought his wife Berenice and his infant son Edmond to the area along with about thirty-five men who were to deal with the trappers and help transport furs to St. Louis. This was the start of Kansas City.

In 1831, Mormons bought some of the land that would become the Country Club Plaza. Mormon Bishop Edward Partridge purchased two plots of land. One stretched along Brush Creek to Ward Parkway and included what is now Loose Park. The other Mormon land was a sixty-acre area just east of 51st and Main. (In the latter area J.C. Nichols would make his first Plaza land purchase in 1905.) The Mormon's stay was short. Within two years the sect's aggressive attempts to convert all of Jackson County to their beliefs resulted in resistant settlers, armed with guns and pitchforks, rousting them off their lands in Brush Creek Valley and out of Jackson County.

Freight wagons bound for the Southwest would next cross the Plaza land. By 1845, the origin of the Santa Fe trade had shifted to Chouteau's Landing at the foot of Grand Avenue on the river. Here, daily steamboats unloaded goods to be traded. The volume of the trade grew to such proportions that freight wagon trains, sometimes three miles long, would leave the levee bound for Santa Fe. The wagons, pulled by oxen and mules, wound their way up the twisted hills south of the levee, and across the unpredictable Ox Creek (where train tracks leading to Union Station now lie). The wagons continued their steady climb until they turned west to cross over into Indian territory. The crossover point changed depending on flooding creeks, the weather, the conditions of the road or simply the preference of the wagonmaster.

Some wagons cut directly west through the town of Westport while others plodded south across Brush Creek and up Wornall hill. One trail led through Loose Park to State Line. The wagoners would stop at a spring near 57th and State Line for a welcome drink of water. It and another trail down Wornall Road led to the town of Dallas (now 103rd and State Line) where the crossover west was made.

The Civil War stopped the Santa Fe trade. The Battle of Westport, the biggest land battle west of the Mississippi, was fought on the Plaza's doorstep and involved 30,000 soldiers. The north banks of Brush Creek provided a staging area for the Union Army while the land across the creek and along Wornall west to State Line became a battleground. The Wornall house, still standing at 61st Terrace and Wornall Road, served as a hospital for the wounded of both sides.

By October 22, 1864, the Confederate forces had pushed the Union troops southwest up the Blue River beyond Independence to Byram's Ford (near the east side of what is now Swope Park). The rebels advanced toward Westport and the levee town of Kansas City, hoping to get the supplies and arms necessary to take Fort Leavenworth.

By sunrise, Sunday, October 23, only the heavy timber of Brush Creek Valley separated the two armies. The army of the South was fortified on the bluffs to the south of the creek. In Westport, less than a mile to the north, people were standing atop the Harris House Hotel ready to watch the all-day battle to be fought in what is now Loose Park and along Wornall Road.

After daybreak the Union forces waded into ice-coated Brush Creek and pushed through the timber hoping to scale the bluffs and push back the invading soldiers. But the Confederate forces, positioned above, had the advantage and repeatedly drove them back into the creek. It seemed to be a lost cause until a farmer from Westport, disgruntled because the rebels had stolen his horse, showed General Samuel Curtis, commander of the Union troops, a narrow gulch (now Rockwell Land) that led just southwest of the Bent farm. (The Seth Ward house, just east of 55th & State Line, is located on what was a portion of that farm.) The troops made their way up the ravine and, emerging behind the Confederate line, took them totally unaware. Although this was the turning point in the battle, the resistance was heavy with forty cannons booming and hand-to-hand fighting lasting into the night. Finally the rebels retreated southward in such great haste that they were forced to leave their dead unburied.

The price of victory was high. The battlefield above Brush Creek was full of the debris of warfare: dead soldiers and horses, shattered weapons and wagons. A conservative estimate was that 3,000 were killed or severely wounded on both sides in the October 23rd action. Some of the dead were buried in a mass grave on the Seth Ward Property just west of Loose Park.

During the 19th Century thousands of people had been participants in the historic dramas played out on the stage of Brush Creek Valley. At the turn of the 20th Century one man would give Brush Creek Valley a new direction and a new identity.

This photograph of J. C. Nichols is taken from his fraternity photograph (Beta Theta Pi) in the 1901 "Jayhawker" yearbook from the University of Kansas.

6

The Man

Just who was this man, J.C. Nichols? And what did he, a few years off the farm, know about developing land into what urban historians acknowledge is one of the most successful commercial developments in the country? How did he gain the artistic perspective to plan and build the Plaza, known around the world for its architecture, sculpture and fountains?

Few would argue with the characterization of J.C. Nichols as an almost compulsive visionary. With a talent for organization and selecting the right people to work for him, Nichols was open to new ideas and willing to risk failure. But underlying it all was an ability to sell himself and his dreams. The seeds had been sown early in life. As a young boy he honed his sales skills by coming up with an endless list of ideas to make money.

Jesse Clyde Nichols was born on a farm outside Olathe, Kansas, on August 23, 1880. Olathe, southwest of Kansas City, had been owned by the Shawnee Indians until the federal government took it over and moved the Indians further west. (The name "Olathe" means "beautiful" in Shawnee.) Olathe, on the path of the great western migration, was the first stopping place for wagons and stagecoaches heading out of Kansas City for Santa Fe.

His father, Jesse Thomas Nichols, was born in 1847 near St. Charlesville, Ohio. He came to Johnson County, Kansas, after serving as a private in the army of the North. His mother, Joanna Jackson, was born in Marietta, Georgia, where at age nine she watched as the troops of General William Tecumseh Sherman burned her house to the ground. Her family later came to Johnson County where she met Jesse Nichols. They were married in 1873.

Kansas City's Union Depot, constructed in 1878, was originally located in the West Bottoms.

They lived on a 220-acre farm just northwest of Olathe where Jesse Clyde and his sister Maude were born. Besides running the farm, his father was the manager of the local Grange store. (He would later be elected County Treasurer.) The Grange, a political association established to help farmers correct economic abuses, also ran small town stores that gave farmers credit so they could buy supplies when they didn't have cash. The elder Nichols also

His son started working at the Grange store on Saturdays when he was eight. He made friends with farmers who came there (some of whom would invest in his early real estate projects). Their conversation about politics and how to make money from what they produced was lively. At age eight, he charged farmers near his home fifty cents a month to bring their cows to and from pasture every day. In fact, J.C. Nichols always seemed to have a job. While still in grade school he worked as a dishwasher in a restaurant, clerked in a drygoods store, and worked for a bakery. At sixteen he was in a business on his own. He purchased a wagon and a team of old horses and, buying chickens, eggs, butter and apples from surrounding farms, took them twenty-five miles to Kansas City. He sold them to restaurants and grocery stores there and bought bananas, oranges and lemons to sell to the people in the country, making profit at both ends of his route.

It was more than spending money. He wanted to earn his way. "I was deeply impressed by the manner in which my parents and grandparents worked hard and I was fired by a deep desire to do my part," J.C. Nichols said later in his life.

His academic work did not suffer from all of this. At Olathe High School he organized the first debating team and the first football team. He graduated in 1897 with a 99.2 average and was valedictorian of his class.

Although his family had the money to pay for his education, Jesse (or Clyde as he liked to be called in school) decided to take a year off to earn his college tuition. He opened a wholesale meat company in Kansas City at 1611 Grand. Nichols contracted with farmers in Olathe to send their meat products by train to the old Union Depot in the west bottoms. Having met the 6 p.m. train, he took the meat to his store and packaged it for early morning delivery. He slept behind a canvas curtain in a corner of his store. Starting with one wagon and a team of mules, by year's end he had five wagons, several employees and contracts with the city's best hotels and restaurants. He also had made enough money to pay for his first year at the University of Kansas in Lawrence.

There, too, Nichols' compulsion to work had him earning money, managing a wholesale meat business, running his fraternity's dining room and taking charge of the University Athletic Association. (He got the latter out of debt for the first time.) He was also a correspondent for *The Kansas City Star*.

College vacations weren't lazy days in the sun. The first summer he loaded potatoes into railroad cars in Kansas City's west bottoms at $1.50 per car. Between his sophomore and junior years he sold maps door-to-door in Utah and Wyoming. Once in a saloon in Wyoming he stood on a whisky keg, and in twenty minutes, sold nineteen maps for a dollar each. When he got tired of map selling, he took a job as a gun-carrying deputy U.S. marshal and chased down lawbreakers in the Southwest.

The next summer's adventure had a lasting influence on him and, as it turned out, the future of Brush Creek. He and a friend worked their way to Europe aboard a cattle boat. They toured Britain and the Continent on bicycles earning money as they went, sometimes singing in a city's public square and passing a hat. The young men often slept in barns and haystacks. Nichols returned to Kansas City with only six cents in his pocket and had to sell his sweater at Union Depot to get enough money to make it home to Olathe.

"The three-month trip made a lasting impression on me," he wrote in his unfinished autobiography. "I was struck most forcefully with the imposing plans and permanent character of the cities and the buildings. I believe that it was then that the spark was struck that ultimately brought the County Club District into being."

In his senior year at K.U., his fellow students recognized his talent for organization and elected Nichols president of his class. He graduated Phi Beta Kappa in 1902, with grades so impressive that Harvard Law School awarded him a scholarship.

Once there, he decided to spend a year studying economics before going into law. His economics professor gave lectures about the shifting patterns of future populations and the potential of undeveloped land resources. The economics classes captured his imagination and law was forgotten. Nichols became so interested in the development and management of land that he wrote his thesis on the subject.

He felt that there was potential in developing sub-marginal land in the southwest United States because he believed that populations would shift toward the sun states. Traveling the Southwest and Mexico looking at this land, he tried to interest investors in developing it for future use. The scheme failed, but traveling in that part of the country gave him insights that would be of use later.

"I think that the seed for a lot of my interest in Spanish-American architecture was sowed during my year in the Southwest," Nichols said. Trying to raise money for the project he took many of his Olathe farmer friends and his future father-in-law, banker M.G. Miller, to the Southwest. But they weren't interested in the project.

If the toss of the coin had been different, there might not have been a Country Club District. Discouraged with the lack of investor interest, Nichols, sitting in a Fort Worth hotel one evening, decided to flip a coin. Heads he would continue to try to sell his idea, tails he would return home. The coin indicated that he should go back to Olathe.

It was a move that would launch his life's work. Back home he had a chance meeting with two K.U. fraternity brothers. They told him about some land in Kansas City, Kansas, near 13th and Lathrop, that was going up for forced bankruptcy sale. They were willing to invest a bit to help buy it if he could raise the money to build small houses on the land and would manage the project. This was the start of J.C. Nichols, developer: "I knew nothing whatsoever about building houses but went back to Olathe, organized a syndicate of investors that included farmers and my future father-in-law, and bought the land."

This was shortly before the 1903 flood. The waters of the Kaw River had not only destroyed many of the businesses in the Kansas bottom lands, but had also taken away most of the houses there. Nichols was at the right place at the right time. His land was on high ground. With an advertising sense that he would later use to promote the Country Club District, Nichols named the land "The Highlands" and printed brochures offering flood victims houses safe from flooding. Each day from 5 a.m. until 6 p.m. he worked on the site with his building crew. From 7 p.m. until 10 p.m. he sold houses to people who wanted to get away from the flood plain. At $800 to $1,000 per parcel of land, he did a brisk business. At the end of that year he paid back his investors and the next year gave them a 65 per cent profit. At age twenty-five, Nichols had tasted success and was ready for bigger things.

Nichols, influenced by his Harvard economics classes, was still a student of land use and population patterns. He had been studying Kansas City, Missouri's growth and saw that as people became more affluent they left old neighborhoods looking for more space and elegant homes. The undeveloped land south of the city limits offered the space to build fine homes for the growing number of people who were getting wealthy off Kansas City's prosperity.

J.C. Nichols decided to invest his "Highlands" profits in land just beyond the city limits. In the spring of 1905, his company bought ten acres of land at 51st and Grand, a few blocks south and east of today's Plaza. This was the start of the Country Club District and its Plaza.

The disastrous flood of Friday, May 29, 1903, left an estimated 15-20,000 people homeless and caused about $90 million in property damages. Water service was cut off and martial law declared. The flood influenced the decision not to build Union Station in the West Bottoms.

Emery Bird Thayer Department Store was a principal business on 11th Street between Main and Walnut when this photo was taken in 1897. The store had started as Bullens, Moore and Emery.

The City

By the time of Nichols' birth in 1880, Kansas City, Missouri, with the help of the railroads, had developed from a modest little town at the levee into a prosperous major city. Kansas City had become a railway center second only to Chicago and the transportation possibilities attracted businessmen from all over the world.

The 1885 Bureau of Statistics reported: "Commercial growth of Kansas City is without parallel in America."

By the mid-1880s twenty-two railroads were shipping freight out of the city. Trains traveling east transported Kansas wheat, cattle from Texas, sheep from Nebraska, corn from Iowa, silver from the rich mining regions of Colorado, Mexico, Utah and Montana and goods manufactured in Kansas City. Trains going west and south carried meat and farm products, as well as such Kansas City goods as flour and hardware. The city was fast becoming the butcher, miller and distributor for a large part of the country.

The Kansas City Stockyards, seen here in 1890, supported a thriving meat-packing industry.

The stockyards covered 140 acres in the west bottoms and there were four major meat packing companies working their employees, mostly immigrants, around the clock to supply the nation's demand. There were seven grain elevators and flour mills operating at full capacity. A steel mill that opened in 1887 in the Blue Valley Industrial District east of town attracted other businesses needing steel as a raw material. Soon the Blue Valley area would be referred to as "Little Pittsburgh."

A total of 1,000 new businesses opened in Kansas City in 1887, adding $10 million in capital to the city. Between 1880 and 1890, property worth $295 million changed hands. The demand for land to build stores, factories, warehouses and homes caused a real estate boom that made fortunes for investors.

In the 1887 City Directory there was a category for "Capitalist" and it had 250 names listed! Six breweries and 300 saloons kept the beer flowing. In 1887, the town had built its first skyscraper, the ten-story New York Life Building at 9th and Baltimore.

The fortunes to be made attracted people from all over the country and the city limits expanded to make room. At the beginning of the 1880s most of the city's population lived in and around the business district close to the river. Many of the wealthy had already moved to Quality Hill, a refined area above the west bluffs that some called "Silk Stocking Ridge." By the middle of the decade those who wanted to show their social status pushed east, building fancy homes along 8th and 9th Streets and Independence Avenue.

The 1890-91 Blue Book, the social register of the time, devoted three pages to the movers and shakers who lived along Independence Avenue. Their two-to-a-block mansions included stables, tennis and croquet courts, extensive gardens and walls of sculptured stone. Mansions were also built along Gladstone Boulevard. (Gladstone, north of Independence Avenue would be the location that lumberman R.A. Long would choose for his seventy-room mansion built in 1911. It now houses the Kansas City Museum.)

Lumber baron R. A. Long's 70-room mansion on Gladstone Boulevard became the Kansas City Musuem of History and Science in 1919.

By the turn of the century the wealthy, seeking newer and better addresses, began to leave their homes on Independence Avenue and move to the fashionable Hyde Park area south of 35th Street. It was here that Fred Harvey, operator of the railroad restaurants, lived as well as the owners of the Armour Meat Packing Company and the prominent architect Louis Curtiss. Living in this neighborhood was a social asset. Adding to the prestige was Hyde Park's Janssen Place, planned by Arthur Stilwell, who dreamed of building a railroad from Kansas City through Mexico. Janssen Place, the city's first restricted residential area, had a private gate leading to mansions designed to reflect the wealth of their owners. Many of these mansions survive today.

Studying this southward movement led to J.D. Nichols' decision to buy land south of the city limits. But perhaps the greatest influence was William Rockhill Nelson's acquisition and development of large acreage to the south of Hyde Park.

Nelson, publisher of The Kansas City Star, had begun to acquire the land in the 1890s. Nelson's original holdings of six city blocks gradually expanded to 275 acres from Locust to Troost and from 44th to what is today Pierce Street on the UMKC campus. In 1887, he constructed his home, Oak Hall, on the site of today's Nelson-Atkins Museum of Art. (In his will he left 20 acres to build an art gallery and stipulated that Oak Hall be razed.)

He and Nichols had some common interests. They both believed in Kansas City and the need for citizen participation in its growth. Nelson did it through his editorials and news coverage in The Star. Nichols, as a civic leader, headed committees, raised money for public projects such as Union Station, and brought his organizational skills to such groups as the Kansas City School Board.

Both Nelson and Nichols believed that community life was enriched when home owners had beautiful surroundings that gave them pride in where they lived. Nelson landscaped his developments with trees and shrubs and built low limestone walls around his houses. Nichols purchased sculpture and fountains to put in his residential neighborhoods.

Foreseeing the importance of the motor car to family life, Nelson built roads through his districts. Nichols planned not only his neighborhoods but his shopping centers with automobile traffic in mind, putting in wide streets and parking areas.

Nelson's promotion and support led to what today is still considered one of the finest parks and boulevard systems in the country, making use of Kansas City's natural scenic topography. One of the most beautiful boulevards, Ward Parkway, came about because Nichols persuaded the Ward family to give the land to the city. He helped lay it out, landscaped it with trees and gardens, and made gifts of many sculpture pieces and fountains to be placed along its route. Carrying the message of the need to put beauty into the urban environment, Nichols became a spokesperson for city planning across the nation.

Nichols understood the importance of the automobile and incorporated wide streets in the Plaza. The building at left is now the Raphael Hotel.

Nelson, a former Indiana building contractor, designed many homes in his districts. In the South Moreland District he built grand houses and mansions, but in the Rockhill District he constructed small frame and stone houses that he used primarily as rental property for his employees. He built Rockhill Road at his own expense, but lobbied the city to bring Warwick and Grand into the area.

By 1897, the southern city limit was 49th Street. A streetcar connection from downtown through Westport brought people to Nelson's neighborhoods and right to the banks of Brush Creek close to 48th and Rockhill. Constructing a stone bridge across the creek (he said he hated iron bridges), Nelson extended Rockhill Road south, then west from 51st Street to the entrance of the Kansas City Country Club and its polo field at 57th and Wornall.

The golf course was laid out in the 1890s on land we now know as Loose Park. Social status was the criteria for membership in the Kansas City Country Club. To play golf, polo or attend dinner at the Club, it meant one had to travel through Nelson's property. The Club's proximity gave Nelson a selling tool. Those wishing to climb the social ladder could buy a house in the South Moreland or Rockhill Districts and live close by the Club.

When Jesse Clyde Nichols bought the property at 51st and Grand in 1905, he was following Nelson's lead in recognizing that young middle-class families who were coming up in the world wanted to live in new neighborhoods with pleasing surroundings and opportunities to socialize with neighbors who were also on the road to success.

The route to the Club passed by Nichol's property on 51st Street. That gave his development visibility, status and a name for his project -- The Country Club Plaza.

Golfers tee off at the Kansas City Country Club from which the Plaza takes its name.

J.C. Nichols (left) looks on as his chauffer, Ernest Holt, stokes the fire in a picnic oven at Mission Hills Country Club. Miller Nichols and his sister, Eleanor, sit foreground while their brother, Clyde, surveys the action from his elevated perch.

EDWARD
BVEHLER
DELK
ARCHITECT
1922

18

The Dream

Brush Creek's path has been straightened over the years. The creek bed once zig-zagged through where the Plaza shops are now. Normally a benign stream, the creek's flooding made a marsh out of the land in the rainy season.

The reputation of the area as a swamp may have saved it from being used for any large development prior to Nichols' arrival on the scene. During the real estate boom of the late 1880s it was surveyed and platted by an enterprising promoter and sold by mail in twenty-five-foot lots to speculators across the country. Most of the buyers never saw their land or did anything with it. At the turn of the 20th Century it was literally a dumping ground.

What land wasn't covered with rubbish was used for a hog farm, a cider mill, a lumberyard, a dairy, a brickyard and a stone quarry. Razor Park, an abandoned Black amusement park, was at Main and Ward Parkway. Rundown shacks were all over the area, including one used for a grocery store where the Plaza Theatre is now. Mill Creek, so named because it powered an early-day grain mill in Westport, crossed the land flowing south to Brush Creek. When it flooded, it cut deep gouges that filled with water that stagnated and bred mosquitoes. A twenty-foot deep swamp pond stood at the southeast corner of 47th and Wyandotte. (The creek eventually dried up and only the name remains.) Wornall Road, the main route from Westport, was still an unpaved wagon trail while Main and 47th Streets were narrow dirt paths. Only a visionary could see potential for this wasteland.

Nichols' early associates tell about him standing on the south hills looking down at Brush Creek Valley and seeing it as he wanted to build it. Gone were the dump and swamp. Instead, his intrigue with Spanish architecture conjured ornate towers, gardens with fountains and statues, and buildings with tiled roofs and wrought iron balconies.

This was the vision that he imparted to designer Edward B. Delk, who translated it into a master plan for a Spanish-styled shopping village with stucco buildings, handcrafted doorways and courtyards -- all decorated with colorful terra cotta tiles. Its streets looked more like parks. As it was to be a marketplace, the name, from Spanish, had to be the "Plaza."

Nichols' 1905 land purchase lay to the east on the south side of the creek at 51st and Grand. He called it Rockhill Park because it was so close to William Rockhill Nelson's districts. (At first Nelson was angry that Nichols had used his name without asking him, but later The Star's publisher supported Nichols' developments and they remained friends until Nelson's death in 1915.)

Nichols and John Taylor, who would eventually become president of the Nichols Company and a key figure in making it run smoothly, made the improvements themselves using horsedrawn scrapers to grade streets and then putting in a wooden sidewalk with lumber they got in exchange for tearing down an old barn at 26th and Grand. Yet none of their improvements could hide from visitors the view of the sordid valley below.

Tracks that once carried city commuters through the Country Club District can still be seen today.

But come they did. Nichols would meet prospective buyers with horse and buggy at the end of the Rockhill streetcar line at 47th and Troost and take them on a tour of the development. He was such a successful salesman that he sold houses in spite of the view. He even sold the house he had intended for his bride, Jessie Eleanor Miller. (They would have three children: Miller, Eleanor, and Clyde.)

Nichols' go-getter ability for real estate development and sales was beginning to attract the attention of the area's more prominent citizens. At age 28, he was asked to join the board of directors at Commerce Bank, becoming its youngest member. The Nichols Company had also gained new investors, grain merchants who had money to back new projects. By 1908, only three years after Nichols' first purchase in the area, his company had acquired or was managing over 1,000 acres of land adjacent to his original holdings. The company now controlled land as far south as 63rd Street and west to the state line. At this time Nichols paid $75,000 for some land in Kansas. (In those days people didn't want to live in Kansas, so land there was cheap.) The area he bought for less than $300 an acre is now Mission Hills, with a national reputation for its millionaires' homes.

Gaining additional land in 1908 gave Nichols even more reason to be concerned about the future of the land north of Brush Creek. Some of the best known families in Kansas City's financial and cultural circles were showing interest in moving south but they had to cross through the valley to get there. Keeping them upwind of the stench of the hog farm was difficult enough, but what if manufacturers came in bringing smokestacks that spewed toxic fumes or coal yards that filled the sky with black dust?

To protect his investment and to create a gateway to the fine homes that he was planning to build, he started buying property along the north side of the creek as early as 1907. It took awhile to assemble the land that was to become the Plaza. Because of the earlier "land by mail" scheme, deeds were hard to trace. Locating owners or their heirs required correspondence and travel to all parts of the world. In one case, an owner was traced to India. But piece by piece, land was purchased until 55 acres were accumulated at a cost of over $1 million.

While this was happening, Nichols was building and selling houses and acquiring more land. Recognizing very early that close-by shops help sell new houses, he built his first shopping center, the Colonial Shops at 51st and Brookside. Although really only a few stores at the end of the Country Club Streetcar Line (which he helped finance as well), the grocery store, meat market, drug store and plumbing outlet provided services sought by residents. The suburban shopping center, small as it was, had arrived.

As the Nichols Company bought more land to the south, the streetcar line was extended. He built shops along its route at 55th and Oak and at 63rd and Brookside. Still remaining today, the shops on 55th Street in the Colonial style and the Tudor design of the 63rd Street buildings, are examples of Nichols' interest in European architecture.

When the plans for the construction of the Plaza were announced April 30, 1922, the story got almost a full page in The Kansas City Star real estate section. The headline was "Millions in New Shops." Some of the city's leaders called it "Nichols' Folly." It may have been inspired by Nichols' vision, but behind the announcement were years of practical planning utilizing all that he had been learning about why people moved to the Country Club District and what they wanted in their community. The plan reflected a study of shopping areas around the world and the input of George Kessler, the landscape architect who had designed Kansas City's park and boulevard system.

The Colonial Shops at 55th and Brookside, seen here in 1920, preceded the Plaza as Nichols' first business development.

To unify the appearance of the entire Plaza, Nichols had his architects and landscape designers plan the whole project in advance so that all future buildings would be part of one harmonious environment. The plan called for theaters, music halls, art studios and refreshment shops. Although some basic changes were made over the years, today's Plaza streets and many of its buildings can be found in the original master plan as painted by Edward Delk in 1922.

The Plaza was designed with the car in mind. Although full of Old-World atmosphere, it offered shoppers every modern convenience. Nichols was before his time in seeing that people would want to shop near their homes. New cars were selling for as low as $395 and families living in the Country Club could afford them. It was a selling point he stressed in advertising Country Club homes; "Only 20 minutes away from Downtown by car."

Plaza streets were wide, sixty feet or more, to permit diagonal parking. Parking lots weren't in the original plan but were soon added. They were to be paved and lighted. By sinking the lots three feet below sidewalk level, parked cars did not obstruct the view of shop windows. Also given the Spanish treatment, they were enclosed inside terra cotta walls and had antique wrought iron gates. On the street side they were landscaped with gardens, statues and fountains.

An early unpaved parking lot was located where Halls now stands. Even the nine filling stations and two garages built on the Plaza were constructed in the Spanish motif, blending with the overall look. "My father believed that beauty should be a part of everyday life, even a shopping trip," said Miller Nichols, oldest son of the Plaza's builder. He took over running the company when his father died in 1950.

To preserve the illusion of a village, utilities were put underground so that no poles or wires would detract from visual continuity of the lines of the tiles roofs. The original plan called for a public square like those found in the center of towns in Spain and Mexico, but this part of the plan never came about. When writing "The Spanish in Kansas City, Missouri," author Herbert Towner wrote asking J.C. Nichols why he chose Spanish design for the Plaza. His reply in 1949 stated:

> *"The reason we chose Spanish was in order to get variance from our other designs (the Colonial at 55th and the English at 63rd). Then too...I have always felt that Kansas City, to a certain extent, was a gateway to all that Southwest country. The truth of the matter is, we have sometimes regretted we chose Spanish architecture for the Plaza, because with the present high cost, it takes a good deal of money to build towers and domes and other characteristics of good Spanish design."*

By the fall of 1923, the land north of Brush Creek had been cleared and graded and ground was broken for construction of the first Plaza building. The two-story structure located at Mill Creek and 47th Street would, according to designer Delk, "one day provide a unique and imposing entrance way to the Country Club District."

This first building was constructed of stucco, but it was discovered that this material did not hold up well and required a great deal of maintenance. The rest of the buildings would be constructed of brick and, later, of concrete.

The Plaza received its first tenant in March, 1923. A photography studio moved in before the building was finished. Called the Suydam Building after an interior decorator who occupied much of the space, it was later renamed the Mill Creek Building. The Architectural League honored the Suydam Building as the best built in 1923.

While this first building was under construction, J.C. Nichols went abroad to attend the International Housing Conference. During his travels through England and the rest of Europe, he started collecting for his "outdoor art gallery," as he liked to call the art objects he placed around his developments. He bought and shipped more than 100 pieces to Kansas City, including antique statues, vases, columns, sun dials, wellheads, and benches. Some of these he placed near street intersections in his neighborhoods while others were intended for Plaza sites. He gave some of these art objects to the city to be used along boulevards and streets in the south part of town. The rest were retained and augmented for future developments and to replace art pieces that were stolen or vandalized. In his lifetime, he would spend over $1 million on outdoor works of art.

Work was started immediately on two more buildings along 47th street: the Wolferman Building and the Tower Building. The first tower built on the Plaza was capped with a dome of brilliant orange tile. Cathedrals and churches in Spain and Mexico served as models for these and later towers.

The Plaza immediately attracted people. When the Fred Wolferman grocery store opened in January, 1924, at the corner of 47th and Wyandotte, over 10,000 customers visited the facility during its first week. These crowds convinced other merchants to come to the Plaza. Joseph M. Robinson, who had a shoe store downtown, opened a second on the Plaza in 1924. The Robinson Shoe Store was the Plaza's oldest tenant until the company declared bankruptcy in 1988.

Looking southwest from 47th and Main in the 30s, the site of the yet-to-be-built Nichols Fountain is still just a grassy field.

City officials felt that Mill Creek Parkway leading from Westport into the Plaza would never have enough traffic to justify the expense of improving the street. So in 1924, the Nichols Company paid to have it widened and paved. The street is now called J.C. Nichols Parkway. But the city did widen and resurface Main Street leading into the Plaza. The Nichols Company also created Alameda Road angling southwest from 47th to Ward Parkway. Eventually, Alameda was straightened to an east-west street and renamed Nichols Road.

Joggers and walkers love the environment of Mill Creek Park.

With the addition of the Balcony and the Triangle Buildings, the Plaza had grown, by 1925, to five 47th Street buildings, housing 37 businesses and four doctors. The Plaza already had two landmarks -- a tower and the tall chimney from the steam-heating operation of the Chandler Landscaping and Floral Greenhouse. This company had been in the Brush Creek Valley since 1916. Nichols bought the Chandler property in 1928, and leased it to the family who continued to do business at the location for many years. The present Swanson's store and Chandler Court are at the old greenhouse location.

The shops and services offered by tenants on the Plaza were promoted throughout the Country Club District by a homeowner newsletter. Residents could read about their neighbors, get helpful homemaking hints, school news, garden tips and learn what the Plaza shops were offering. They were a captive audience.

But those who lived south weren't the only ones coming to the Plaza. Publicity about the area so excited imaginations that it drew people from all over the area. A transfer downtown to the Country Club streetcar line could get a passenger there from any place in the two Kansas Cities for a dime. One could buy a tasty hotdog and a Coke at Wolferman's counter for twenty-five cents. A stroll around the shops cost nothing, and when the Plaza Theatre opened, matinee tickets were only a dime.

The Chandler Greenhouse chimney (left) was a Plaza landmark for years. The site now accommodates Swanson's.

The Plaza Theatre opened October 9, 1928, at the southeastern corner of 47th and Wyandotte. Its magnificent tower, a replica of one atop a convent in Mexico, and its lavish interior decor rivaled any of the ornate movie palaces being built in Hollywood or New York. Wanting the theater to be authentic in every way, J.C. Nichols and John Taylor went to Spain to personally select art objects. They had to wait three months for the Spanish government's permission to take them out of the country. This Spanish treasure trove included pieces dating back to the 16th-Century: wall hangings from Granada, lighting fixtures from Seville and wellheads from Barcelona. The auditorium, with its barrel-vaulted ceiling modeled after the Palacio de Las Duenas in Seville, was full of grills, balconies, pennants, and lanterns. Spanish scenes were painted in the balcony alcoves and atop the floors of colorful mosaic tiles were laid beautiful Moorish rugs. Antique statues decorated the lobby and downstairs lounges.

A large lobby fountain covered with more mosaic tiles was later removed to make way for a refreshment stand. The theater's interior was changed drastically in the 1970s when it was cut up and made into three small-screen movie theaters.

The stage had been designed to accommodate live entertainment. (It would hold the Kansas City Philharmonic when that group played matinee concerts there in the 1960s.) The theater, built the year before sound came to the movies, was home to the second largest theater organ in town. It provided pre-show entertainment and sound effects during the silent "flickers." Architect Edward Tanner's design made it easy to add sound equipment when the "talkies" arrived. The building won an award from the Architectural League as the best built that year.

The bones and fossilized remains of long-extinct animals have been unearthed throughout the Kansas City area. Eons ago, a saltwater sea covered the area. Rising and falling many times, the water trapped tiny creatures whose fossils form the limestone cliffs on the south side of the Missouri River. At various building sites in Kansas City, workers have uncovered the bones of such creatures as a mammoth, a bear, giant elk and sea serpents.

In April, 1928, while excavating the foundation of the Plaza Theatre at 47th and Wyandotte, workmen came upon a tooth over five inches wide. With its enamel still intact, the tooth was almost perfectly preserved. The molar weighed two and a half pounds and had roots over four inches long. A University of Kansas paleontologist said it had once belonged to a mastodon. Judging by the fossil record, we are only the latest in a long line of inhabitants at this place we call Kansas City.

Each new building brought more to do and more to see on the Plaza. For the locals it was a one-day vacation. Out-of-town visitors had to see the Plaza before they left. One wonders what kind of a tourist town Kansas City would have been without it. In the early years visitors not only came to look at the Spanish buildings and towers, but to watch people on horseback at the riding academy on the southeast corner of Pennsylvania and Nichols Road. (There were riding trails throughout the Country Club District and horse owners stabled their horses at the academy.)

For children, there was a pony ring across the street at Pennsylvania and Nichols Road where later there would be a Woolworth dime store and -- still later -- the Saks Fifth Avenue of today. A miniature golf course was later added in a hollow on the south side of Nichols Road near Broadway where Jack Henry Clothing is now. During the Christmas season, a little house in the hollow was equipped with a loudspeaker that "Santa" would use to talk to children who came to see him.

The Plaza Theatre's decor was supervised by J.C. Nichols, who imported Spanish art for its interior. The theater opened a year before "The Jazz Singer" ushered in sound.

The Kansas City Museum at Corinthian Hall is now the repository for this mammoth's tooth, which was unearthed during the excavation for the Plaza Theatre.

Even in the 1940s, the Plaza's lights reflected the splendor that has become their hallmark.

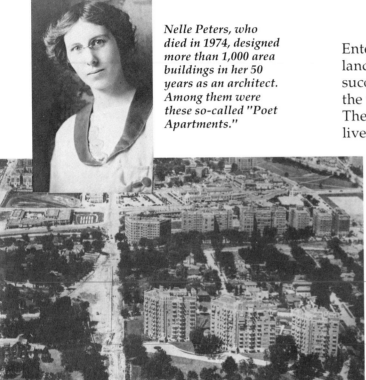

Nelle Peters, who died in 1974, designed more than 1,000 area buildings in her 50 years as an architect. Among them were these so-called "Poet Apartments."

Built in 1929, the Walnuts remain one of the city's most prestigious addresses. Doorman L.C. Mosley welcomes residents.

The famous Plaza Christmas lights had their genesis in 1925. Like most Christmas traditions, they started small with a single strand of colored lights hung above the door of the Suydam Building. Today, the lights outline building rooflines throughout the Plaza in the tradition known world-wide.

It didn't take long for the Plaza, the first major suburban shopping center, to gain international recognition. From the very beginning, it attracted architects and builders who sought to emulate its success.

Enterprising developers, realizing that the Nichols company did not own all the land in the Brush Creek Valley, were eager to ride on the coattails of the Plaza's success. If one imagines the Plaza as occupying the center of a bowl nestled in the valley, the circle surrounding that basin was owned by other developers. There was money to be made in building apartments for people who wanted to live near the Plaza. The first apartments were built along the north side of 47th Street west from Broadway. Just before the Great Depression, apartment construction began at several Plaza locations. Just east at 46th and Main the Ponce de Leon Apartments were built in 1929. Building also began that year on a group of 13 apartments on the southwest side of the Plaza in the 48th and Ward Parkway/Roanoke area.

Designed by Mrs. Nelle Peters, much-admired architect of the period, some of the apartments were named after American poets and are fondly referred to as "the poet apartments." On the hillside just south of the Creek six apartment buildings with a total of 550 units were built along Ward Parkway by the McCanles Building Company. The Villa Serena (which became the Raphael Hotel), the Lacarno, the Riviera (where Ernest Hemingway lived for a time in the 1920s), the Biarritz and the two Casa Lomas were intended to attract those who could afford a higher-priced lifestyle.

But the ultimate in apartment living could be found up the hill and a few blocks south of 50th and Wornall. The Walnuts, three 10-story apartment high-rises, begun in 1929 and completed the next year, catered to those wealthy and socially connected people who wanted to live near the Plaza. Situated on spacious grounds and offering every luxury, they remain one of the city's most prestigious addresses.

One didn't have to be wealthy to live on the Plaza. The 1929 newspaper want ads listed five-room apartments in the area for as low as $50 a month. With the abundance of apartments encircling the area, even office workers or shop girls could share the cost and have a home in the Country Club Plaza.

Another parcel of land not owned by the Nichols Company was 48th Street from Pennsylvania to Jefferson, on the southwest end of the development. For a long time stores on this street traded on the Plaza name without paying money to the Nichols Company. Small shops including paint stores, a shoe shop, cleaners, a pet store and a bar and restaurant occupied this street until the 1977 flood. That deluge and a fire wiped out these businesses for good. The street now belongs to the Nichols Company.

The Depression years slowed down the company's residential sales. They showed a profit in only one year between 1929 and 1936. But they managed to keep all their employees working aided by rents from Plaza merchants and tenants. In 1937, with the completion of the Plaza Medical Building, more doctors and dentists moved their practices to the Plaza. The area gained additional tenants and a new tower.

The money crunch of the Depression made the merchants aware that they had to do more than open their shops every morning to attract customers. The Merchants Association came up with a variety of activities to attract people to the Plaza during the 1930s. In 1932, it organized the first Plaza Art Fair. Held on an empty lot at Nichols Road and Center, artists displayed their paintings by leaning them against trees and benches.

People couldn't afford to go away on vacations but they could go to the Plaza. Cooking schools held there attracted 3,000 persons a month. Over 2,000 women showed up for weekly book reviews. There were crowds for flower and fashion shows and people even turned out in numbers for contract bridge classes. The first Spanish Fiesta, in 1936, attracted 20,000 people over a two-day period. The merchants and their employees dressed in colorful Spanish costumes. The food, music, and dancing were so appreciated by Depression-limited travelers that the event was repeated for several years.

An event of another kind happened on the Plaza in the 1930s. The Brush Creek Sewer Project brought an army of men into the Plaza area to reroute the creek and pave it over with massive slabs of concrete. During 1936 and 1937, shoppers and Plaza visitors were treated to a daily spectacle of men with picks and shovels, noisy machines, and trucks delivering and pouring concrete. Some Country Club residents felt that the beauty of Brush Creek was being completely destroyed by this invasion. It was bad enough putting up with the noise, dust and disruption of traffic and they did not appreciate being in the center of a controversy surrounding the project.

The Spanish Fiesta during the late 1930s drew large crowds of Depression-era Kansas Citians looking for a momentary escape from their economic woes.

The Plaza Art Fair has established an annual presence on the Plaza.

27

Tom Pendergast

The paving of Brush Creek was part of a $40 million public improvement bond package that included federal money for public works to keep workers employed. It was said that City Manager H.F. McElroy sank an additional $1 million into the bond proposal to pave the creek at the last minute so that more of political boss Thomas Pendergast's ready mix concrete could be used (even though plenty was being used in such projects as City Hall, Jackson County Court House, Municipal Auditorium and the Music Hall. All built at the same time, each building used the same brand of concrete.)

Pendergast's concrete has held up through the years, but so has the speculation that Pendergast used his power over city officials.

The Second World War put people back to work and they came to the Plaza to spend their money. Soldiers and sailors on leave came to see the first-run hits at the Plaza Theatre and eat at one of the eight restaurants, including Bo Lings on 48th Street. (The restaurant would remain until it was wiped out in the 1977 flood.) The nine automobile service stations on the Plaza would sell gas only if the customer had the requisite ration stamps issued during the war.

In 1943, when the Plaza Bowl opened on Nichols Road, where Saks Fifth Avenue is today, it became a big success with young and old. Bowling was a popular sport during the war years. J.C. Nichols bowled the first game at the alley. The Bowl's restaurant and cocktail lounge became a popular meeting place. Women would bowl in the afternoons and many tournaments were held there. Later in the 1950s a popular TV bowling show would originate from the Plaza Bowl.

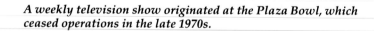

A weekly television show originated at the Plaza Bowl, which ceased operations in the late 1970s.

Anticipating that the automobile industry would start turning out cars for returning veterans, the Nichols Company planned a triple-deck parking lot with a 600-car capacity. Shortly after the war's end, it was built between 47th and Nichols Road at Pennsylvania. The Plaza Time Building was also in the planning stage during the war and was constructed in 1947. Its 104-foot tower with four clock faces is a dominant feature of the Plaza skyline. Thousands of tiles, fired in Mexico, were used in the clocks -- which still keep good time. The Jack Henry Men's Store, the building's main tenant, occupied the corner space. The top floor of the building accommodated forty-two physicians and dentists. The Plaza continues to have a high concentration of medical offices, while an expanded Jack Henry is still doing business on the same corner.

A flurry of building occurred during the late 1940s. In 1947, Sears, Roebuck and Company came to the Plaza. A three-story edifice taking up a half block was constructed on the north side of Nichols Road between Pennsylvania and Jefferson. Sears sold everything from clothes and appliances to car batteries (at the automotive shop across the street). The main building was completely remodeled in the mid-1970s to become Seville Square, now called Seville on the Plaza, an enclosed shopping center. The automotive shop across the street became the Court of the Penguins, a popular grouping of boutiques.

In 1949, Emery, Bird and Thayer moved a branch of its downtown department store to 47th and Broadway. It later became a Macy's store and, when that company pulled out of Kansas City, a Dillard's branch.

On February 16, 1950, J.C. Nichols died of cancer at his home on 55th Street. Modern Kansas City had grown up with this man, a pioneer in city planning and development. He had been a key leader in most of the city's civic enterprises of the first half of the 20th Century. In the planning and building of residential districts and the creation of the Plaza he had helped shape the city. He set standards of quality design and construction that continue to influence builders all over the world. Few men have had the opportunity to realize their dreams in their own lifetimes, but J.C. Nichols did. As Miller Nichols recalled, "My father did have the capacity to dream and to see those dreams come true."

Formerly a Sears department store, Seville on the Plaza now houses theaters, specialty shops and restaurants.

J.C. Nichols had never been satisfied to keep the Plaza's status quo. He always wanted to make it better, and that was the challenge that Miller Nichols inherited. But making the Plaza better meant making sure that it survived.

Suburban lifestyle was catching on all over the country. Land in south Kansas City and to the west and east was being developed into new suburban housing areas. Residents of these areas obviously wished to shop closer to their homes. Shopping centers were going to have to compete with these newer and more accessible shopping areas. (The Nichols Company supplied some of its own competition by building a large shopping center not too far away in Prairie Village, Kansas.)

Emery Bird Thayer Department Store built a Plaza branch in 1949. The building subsequently housed Macy's, then Dillard's Department Stores.

The architecture of the Plaza was unique. Its atmosphere attracted people, but the shops were obliged to offer unique shopping experiences and merchandise not found in other shopping malls. With the addition of the Halls and Swansons stores in the 1960s, the shopping atmosphere of the Plaza began to change. Their success in catering to more affluent buyers made companies on the East and West Coasts look to the Plaza as a new site for their high-fashion stores. Soon, Saks, Gucci, and Brooks Brothers were replacing the Woolworth dime store, the bowling alley and the small shops. To help advance this image, the Nichols Company took over the Sears building and turned it into Seville Square. It boasts a multiplicity of shops under one roof.

The Nichols Company helped bring more customers to these new stores when it built the high-rise Sulgrave and the Regency apartments on Ward Parkway. With the completion of the Alameda Plaza Hotel and the transformation of the Villa Serena apartments into the Raphael Hotel, the Nichols Company guaranteed a tourist trade for the shops and restaurants.

Change is inevitable. It is what history is all about. Change can be man-made, such as turning a swamp into a beautiful Spanish market place. Or it can be natural, happening without warning and resulting in chaos.

On September 12, 1977, an old enemy came to call on the Country Club Plaza. The waters of Brush Creek rose over its banks and flooded the area. It was called the 1,000 year's flood. Water, it is said, has a memory. The water took its old paths through the valley, flooding long-dried-up creek beds including the old Brookside waterway south from Volker Boulevard and reclaiming its rights on the Plaza as well.

Brush Creek, the stream that usually was only a few inches deep, became a wall of water, moving down the paved channel at a height of fifteen to twenty feet. At 11:30 p.m. on that Monday evening in 1977, the water came over the creek's banks and inundated the Plaza.

The water moved everything in its wake. Shop windows caved in. Parked cars were swept into trees and windows, or carried along with the swiftly moving water to be wedged under bridges. In the aftermath, thirty-five wrecked cars were towed from the creek, the Plaza tennis courts, and sidewalks. The powerful surge of water destroyed statuary and other art works. It blew holes in walls and twisted off the massive wooden doors of Halls, carrying them away as if they had no weight. In the 600 block of 48th Street, the force of the water ripped open a gas line causing an explosion that destroyed that block's shops.

Waters running off higher land south and west of the Plaza surged through the shopping district the night of September 12, 1977, destroying many ground-level shops.

It had come so quickly that many diners at Plaza restaurants refused to leave, thinking they had time to finish their meal. As water came in under doors of the Plaza III restaurant, customers were finally motivated to get up to leave. But before they made it to the exits, they were wading in waist-high water. In some of the businesses the water level rose to heights of five and seven feet. Heroically, restaurant workers, bus boys, waiters and passersby formed human chains to get people to safety. There were also a few who took it lightly and were seen swimming in the streets of the Plaza.

Although the Plaza was the hardest hit, the greatest loss of life and damage on both sides of the state line came with flood waters from Kansas rushing to join the Blue River. A total of twenty-three lives were lost; many were trapped in their cars. Flooding creeks in Kansas killed people at 89th and State Line and there were drowning deaths in Missouri as far south as 63rd and Rockhill as the waters sought old paths.

The morning light revealed the full extent of the damage to the Plaza. Thirty-five stores were damaged. Water had reached as far north as 47th Street. It was still knee-high in many stores including the first floor of Halls and the basement of the Bennett Schneider bookstore where there was extensive loss. The Alameda ballroom and meeting rooms also were flooded. It was later estimated that the Plaza suffered $58 million in damages and business losses. Some speculated that the Plaza would never recover. But those shops not affected by the catastrophe opened the next day. The life blood of a merchant is being able to sell his merchandise.

The cleanup began that morning and Miller Nichols pledged that the Plaza would be ready for the annual Art Fair due to begin in ten days. People came from everywhere to offer help, reaffirming how much the Plaza meant to them. The merchants, the public and the Nichols Company employees made it possible. The Art Fair was held and acclaimed as the best ever. Christmas that year included the traditional lights. Some heavily damaged stores had to be completely remodeled and couldn't open by Christmas. However, many of the smaller shops, especially those destroyed in the 600 block of 48th Street never reopened.

Built on a swamp, the Plaza had fought the waters a second time and won again. Having battled the water, there was still the continuing challenge to keep the Plaza forever new. Over the past decade the Nichols Company has spent millions adding to and expanding the Plaza. Sixteen towers now grace its horizon. The newest ones (at Ward Parkway and Pennsylvania and at 46th Terrace and Nichols Parkway) carry on the Spanish theme.

Many Kansas Citians have a feeling of ownership about the Plaza. Those who have grown up with it and the new generations who discover it are all proud of this American original known throughout the world. The stone masons, bricklayers, carpenters and other artisans who have helped build it, take pride in knowing that they created something quite unique. Those builders took Nichols' vision from the architects' designs and made it a reality.

Some would say the Plaza had gone beyond its founder's imaginings. But dreams once accomplished only make room for new ones. For J.C. Nichols, dreams were opportunities. He did not limit his vision to the past or present, but planned for the future.

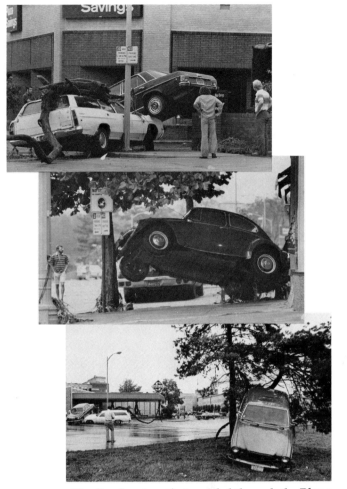

The flood waters that swirled through the Plaza the night of September 12, 1977, swept away vehicles and left them in strange formations.

J.C. Nichols' high school graduation picture, 1898.

J.C. Nichols
Visionary, Planner, Public Servant

J.C. Nichols personified the saying "If you want something done, ask a busy man to do it." While acquiring and developing land, he spent a great deal of time serving on the boards of local and national projects. He didn't just lend his name to a project; he was an active participant. During the last thirty years of his life, at least one third of his time was given to public service. He served eight years on the Kansas City School Board. During the First World War he was either chairman or vice chairman of all the Liberty Loan and Red Cross fund-raising drives. As vice chairman of the committee to build the Liberty Memorial, he and lumberman R.A. Long were given the task of raising the money to build it. The monument, a tribute to those who gave their lives in World War I, remains one of Kansas City's most impressive historical sites and stands as evidence of Nichols' expertise in supervising its planning and overseeing its construction.

Because of his interest in the cultural life of Kansas City, Nichols nurtured many of the arts organizations that prosper today. For example, as one of the three original trustees appointed to administer the William Rockhill Nelson Trust Fund, he helped oversee the millions of dollars that were left to build the Nelson-Atkins Museum and buy art objects to fill it. When Nichols took over as president of the Art Institute in 1920, it was a small operation on the second floor of a building near 12th and McGee. He guided the school through its transition into one of the leading art schools in the country. He served as the vice president of the Kansas City Symphony Orchestra (forerunner of the Kansas City Philharmonic which later became, again, the Kansas City Symphony) and as treasurer for the Conservatory of Music.

Ever interested in bolstering the area's economy, as vice president of the Missouri River Navigation Association, he not only worked hard to improve the river as a commercial shipping lane, but also promoted all of the Midwest's inland waterways. The Midwest Research Institute was conceived by Nichols and he supported it financially in its early years. He felt that this facility, located just east of the Plaza, would attract business and industry to the city. Today the institute is recognized internationally for its innovative approach to solving the complex problems of private and governmental industries.

On the national scene, Nichols was appointed by three different presidents to serve on the seven-member National Capital Park and Planning Commission. Empowered to supervise the improvement and beautification of the District of Columbia, the commission selected the sites and oversaw the building of the Lincoln and Jefferson Memorials and the impressive mall. Nichols served on this commission for twenty-three years. As a leader in the formation of the Urban Land Institute, he worked with many cities on planning and zoning.

In the 1930s he was called by President Franklin Roosevelt to help set up the Federal Housing Administration. In 1940, the President asked him to serve on the Advisory Council for National Defense. Finding that there wasn't a single plant or military airport proposed for the Midwest, Nichols became a one-man lobby in Washington to bring war industry plants to the middle of the country. Because of his efforts, Kansas City got the Lake City ordnance plant, a large quartermaster depot, and the Pratt-Whitney airplane plant. The North American bomber plant was located in Fairfax and Kansas also got the Sunshine ordnance facility. This meant jobs for area workers and increased productivity for the war effort.

J.C. Nichols died February 16, 1950. At his funeral service the Rev. Warren Grafton, pastor of the Country Club Christian Church, said: "If you want to see the monument of J.C. Nichols, look around as you go out the doors of this church. Never did so great a community owe so much to one man." Nichols' community was larger than his Country Club district or the Kansas City area. His contributions influenced the nation. President Harry S. Truman summed it up in his telegram sent to Nichols' widow at the time of his death. The President declared Nichols "a distinguished public servant."

A modest bronze plaque at the entrance to the J. C. Nichols Co. is the only formal tribute to the Plaza's founder. It suggests that those seeking his monument need merely to look about them.

It remained for Miller Nichols, (left), seen here with his father and brother, J.C. and Clyde Nichols, to carry on the Plaza's development.

A son inherits a father's dream

Miller Nichols and the Plaza grew up together. Shortly after the first Plaza building was finished, Miller, J.C. Nichols' oldest son, began to spend his summers working at the company's woodworking mill.

"The mill was in back of what used to be the fire station on 63rd Street in Brookside," Miller said. "I swept up the wood shavings and sawdust. I also glued and sanded the door frames that the carpenters were making. I was twelve years old, worked five and a half days a week and was paid twelve dollars."

Every summer vacation he worked for the company. He watered trees planted in the residential areas, bailed hay for the ninety mules that pulled the street-grading equipment, and, when he was old enough to drive a truck, spent a summer making several runs a day carrying gravel for the Plaza streets from the rock quarry. Later he helped lay the tile floor in the J.C. Nichols office building on Ward Parkway. "You might say I learned the business from the ground up," he says with a chuckle.

After graduating in economics from the University of Kansas in 1934, he started working full-time with the company. "When I hear that young people, after completing college, want to take off a year to 'find themselves,' I tell them it took me all of about twenty minutes," he says. "When I graduated from Kansas University in 1934, my last responsibility was to oversee a luncheon given for the new dean of the college at the Hotel Muehlebach. My father attended the luncheon and needed a ride back to his office. As we were leaving downtown, he asked me what I was going to do next. I thought he meant that afternoon and I told him I thought I'd just go home. He said, "Well you may as well stop by the office now and start to work right away.' My finding myself took only the time required to drive from downtown to the Plaza."

Miller Nichols joined the company's residential sales staff. During the Depression it was not easy selling anything. It took him a year to make his first sale and now, over fifty years later, he can recall the exact location of the house and the people to whom he sold it. He also remembers the impact that the Depression had on the Nichols Company. Every morning at 6 a.m. his father would meet with the department heads around the breakfast table at his home on 55th Street and discuss any problems."

Even the Plaza's gas stations (revenues from which kept the Plaza financially solvent during the Depression) reflected their architectural environment.

I would hear the toll that the Depression was taking on real estate firms across the country," Miller said. "For about five or six years we didn't sell anything except six inches of property to a homeowner who had built too close to a property line. Companies like ours that built better houses were failing everywhere. Only one in New Jersey and our firm survived. We were able to pay our bills. And do you know what made that possible? The nine filling stations on the Plaza. People still needed gas and somehow they could afford it; I think it was about fifteen cents a gallon. The rents we received from those nine stations kept us afloat."

Clyde Nichols, Miller's younger brother, also worked for the company and later formed his own air-conditioning and building organization. Eleanor Nichols, J.C.'s daughter, helped organize the Spanish Fiestas and other activities on the Plaza. She and her husband, Earl Allen, an architect for the Nichols firm, were killed in a tragic fire in the 1960s.

Miller served in both the Army and the Navy in the early 1940s. Drafted into the Army in the spring of 1941, he was soon released because he was over thirty and married. After the bombing of Pearl Harbor, he enlisted in the Navy. While stationed in San Francisco, he met fellow Missourian David Jackson and invited him to contact him after the war. Jackson's background in business and engineering got him a job with the Nichols Company where he worked his way up to become president in 1973.

When J.C. Nichols died in 1950, Miller took over the company. He doesn't remember that challenge as particularly overwhelming, but credits John Taylor, his father's longtime friend and partner, for his advice and counsel.

After the 1977 flood, the many offers of help made him realize how much the Plaza meant to the ordinary citizen. They came from every segment of the city. Men skilled with water pumps and other laborers worked long and hard to get the water out and the damage repaired. Many members of the public also showed up asking what they could do or volunteering to clean the mud out of the shops.

"The people of Kansas City feel that the Plaza belongs to them. And it does. We work hard to do the things that the public wants. I know that we aren't always in agreement. But it's only through change that we can progress."

At seventy-eight, Miller Nichols' life has started to change. Having resigned as chairman of the Nichols Company, he still remains on its board. He says it gives him time to do what he wants, although he goes to the office every day to offer counsel. He especially likes to talk with the new generation of people who have joined the company. "We ask that young people get involved in civic endeavors," he says. "This is a carry-over from my father's commitment to public service."

Miller Nichols still values highly his father's use of art objects outdoors and continues to acquire them for the streets of the residential districts and the Plaza. "Bubbling fountains, sculptures, and colorful paintings all create an ambience of tranquility that's not easy to bring into a busy shopping center," he said. "It's frequently unconscious. Being surrounded by beautiful things is what makes people feel great."

Since early boyhood Miller Nichols has helped build and shape the Country Club Plaza. When asked what he would do with his life if he had to live it all again, he smiled and said: "I'd go into the real estate business."

Postscript

If there is a juncture in recent history that provides us with a point of reference about the Plaza as we know it today, it must certainly be the flood of September 12, 1977. A stalled storm system over Kansas City produced as much as 15 inches of rainfall in 24 hours, causing some of the greatest damage and loss of life since the flood of 1951.

Among the hardest hit areas of the city was the Country Club Plaza where many of the ground-level shops between Brush Creek and J. C. Nichols Parkway were inundated and destroyed. Once the merchants had pumped out the water and swept out the mud, it was apparent that Mother Nature had, in one watery stroke, set in motion a process that resulted in the Plaza as we know it today.

There were no protracted committee planning sessions, only the need to get "up and running" again as quickly as possible. After the shock of the disaster bad subsided, merchants seized upon the opportunity to recreate their businesses bigger, better and more stylish than ever.

The disaster also hastened along a natural transition in consumer-dictated change that demanded a greater focus on fashion, entertainment and restaurants. Saks Fifth Avenue, Brooks Brothers, Gucci, Luara Ashley and Abercrombie & Fitch were among the names that joined the Plaza family of stores, replacing a host of marginal services that had been losing customer patronage over the years. Already a mecca for tourists, the area added other fine eating places such as Fedora's, Bristol Bar & Grill, and Houston's. Whether cutting a deal with a business associate or taking one's date out for a candlelight dinner, the Plaza's eating places offer the appropriate environment.

By the mid-1980s, the tempo of new apartment building construction and rehabilitation of older ones had increased, reaffirming the Plaza's popularity as a residential setting for the young business person as well as the older, more established Kansas Citian. And travelers wanting only a temporary residence have come to rely on the Ritz-Carlton, the Raphael and the other fine hostelries nearby.

As the Plaza has strengthened its image as an elegant center for the sophisticated shopper with the money to indulge his wishes, it has also remained accessible to those who seek quality without intimidating price tags. Tailor-made or off the rack; Chicken McNuggets or veal cordon bleu, the Plaza manages to please a broad-spectrum clientele.

But if one speaks only of a wide assortment of shops offering good merchandise at acceptable prices, he has not yet explained what sets the Plaza apart from its mercantile counterparts at the various suburban malls around the city.

"The people who work and shop here like the way the Plaza makes them feel," suggests one under-thirty sales clerk when asked to explain the district's popularity. Indeed, the sheer physical beauty of the Plaza, reflected in its integrated architectural plan and the use of fine art in its outdoor spaces, imparts a sense of occasion to the visitor. The remembered feeling of well-being is the intangible lure that draws people to the Plaza again and again.

Added to the Plaza's physical assets must be the pervasive good aura that emanates from the personalities who live and work there. A natural Midwestern good-naturedness is abetted by the Plaza's unique ability to put people in good spirits and harmonious temper.

One supposes that if Jesse Clyde Nichols had been able to describe the Plaza of the 1980s to his turn-of-the-century associates, they would have claimed the vision too good to be true. But, with the guidance of his successors, the Plaza continues to fulfill Nichols' dream in an urban evolution of style and grace that is as good as it is true.

-- David S. Hudson, Editor

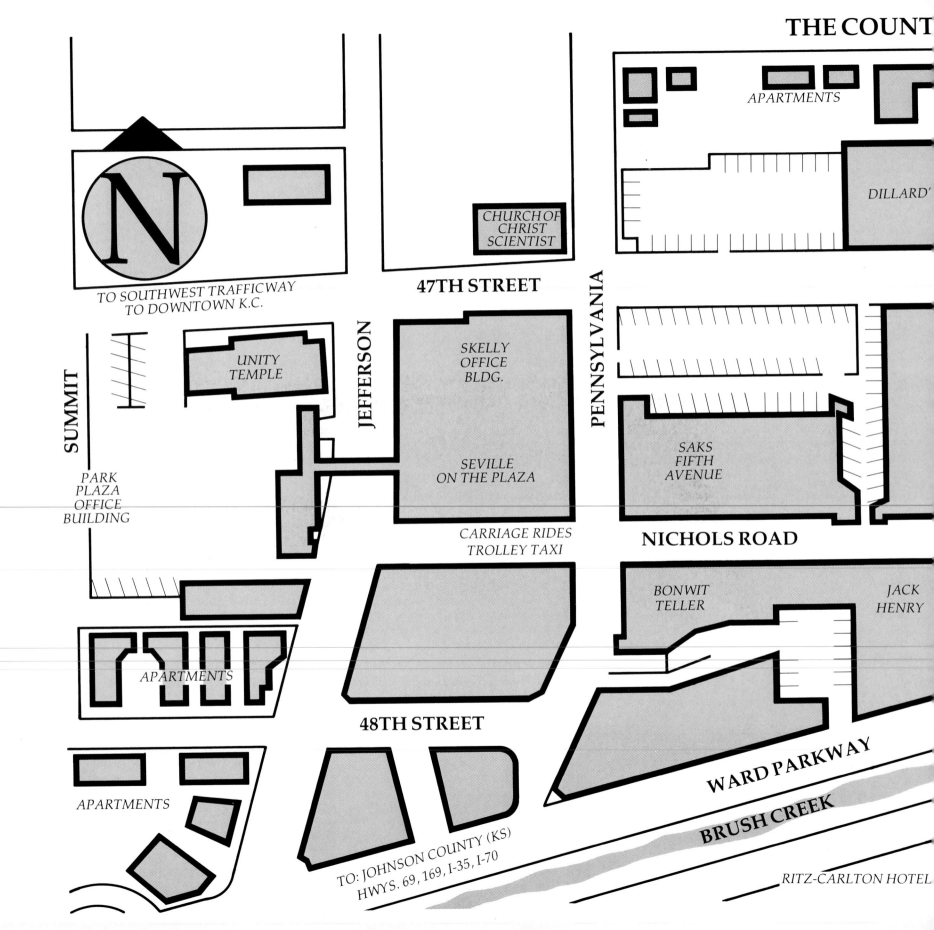

APARTMENTS

DILLARD'

CHURCH OF
CHRIST
SCIENTIST

47TH STREET

PENNSYLVANIA

JEFFERSON

TO SOUTHWEST TRAFFICWAY
TO DOWNTOWN K.C.

UNITY
TEMPLE

SKELLY
OFFICE
BLDG.

SUMMIT

PARK
PLAZA
OFFICE
BUILDING

SEVILLE
ON THE PLAZA

SAKS
FIFTH
AVENUE

CARRIAGE RIDES
TROLLEY TAXI

NICHOLS ROAD

BONWIT
TELLER

JACK
HENRY

APARTMENTS

48TH STREET

WARD PARKWAY

APARTMENTS

TO: JOHNSON COUNTY (KS)
HWYS. 69, 169, I-35, I-70

BRUSH CREEK

RITZ-CARLTON HOTEL

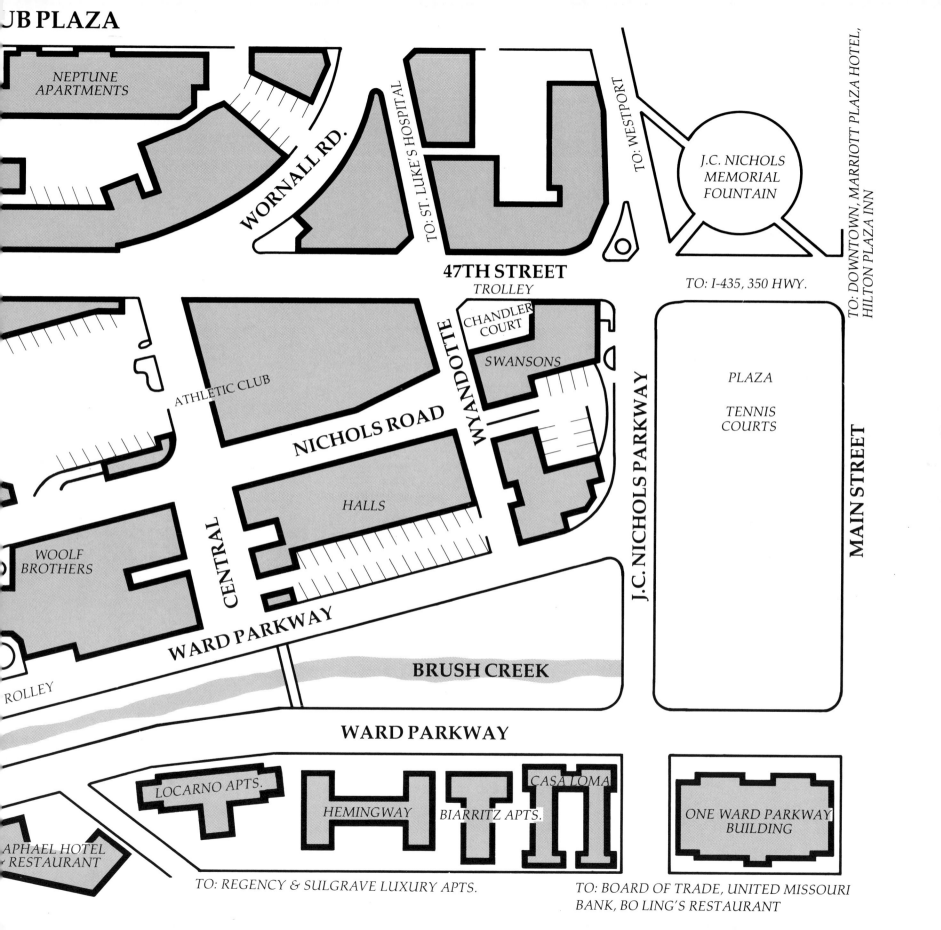

The Plaza is a window-shopper's paradise, with block after block of interesting and attractive window displays throughout the year.

Plaza Merchants

AT&T Phone Center
Abercrombie & Fitch Co.
Absolute Florist
Aca Joe
Alaskan Fur Co.
American Express Travel
American Indian Store
Ann Taylor
Annie's Santa Fe
Asiatica
Athlete's Foot
Au Marché
Bailey Banks & Biddle
Banana Republic
Baskin-Robbins
Benetton
012 Benetton
Bennett Schneider
The Better Cheddar
Bo Ling's
Boatmen's Bank
Bonwit Teller
Bristol Bar & Grill
Brooks Brothers
Bruce Smith Drugs
Cafe Kona Kai
Casual Corner
Caswell-Massey Co., LTD.
Catch Kansas City, Inc.
Ceasare's European Hair
    Fashion
Charade Watches
Christian Science Reading
    Room
Christy's Beauty Salon
The Classic Cup
The Coach Store
Commerce Bank Plaza
Community Federal Savings
Country Club Bank
Crabtree & Evelyn
Creative Hands
Curios
Demaree
Diebel's Sportsmen's
    Gallery
Dillard's
Duvall's
Elizabeth Reed Sweater Shop

Emilie's European Foods
Executive Barber Shop
Farrar's Initmate Apparel
Federal Express
Fedora's Cafe
Fiddler on the Square
Finishings for Her
Fireside on the Plaza
Fred P. Ott's Bar & Grill
Function Junction
The Gap, Inc.
Gerhardt Fur Co.
Gilbert/Robinson
Gourmet Grocer
The Granfalloon Bar & Grill
Grossman Jewelry
Gucci
Hair Care Harmony
Halls Plaza
Helzberg Diamonds
Hibachi Japanese Steak
    House
Hilliard Gallery
Hilton Plaza Inn
Hires
Home Savings & Loan
Houlihan's Old Place
House of Toy
Houston's Restaurant
ID
Ilten Brass
Jack Henry Clothing Co.
Jaeger International
Jenkins Music Co.
Joan Bari
Jordan Windsor
K.C. Coffee & Tea
Kansas City Marriott Plaza
Kansas City Trolley Corp.
Kaplan's Fabrics
Key Largo Surf Club
La Bonne Boucheé
La Mediterraneé French
    Restaurant
Laura Ashley
Laura Ashley for the Home
Leathergear
Let's Party

The Limited
The Linen Shop
Le Papillon Florist
Longbranch Saloon
Lou Charno Photography
    Studio
M. J. Surreys Ltd.
Maillard's
Marge Kregel Travel, Inc.
Maria's Plaza Taylor Shop
Mario's on the Plaza
Maxim Designs Ltd.
McDonald's
Micro Age Computer
    Center
Missouri Memories
Mister Guy
Mrs. Fields Cookies, Inc.
Muehlbach's West
Musicland
N. Valentino
Nabil's Bistro
National 1-hour Photo
J.C. Nichols Realtors &
    Developers
O. H. Gery Optical
One-Hour Photo
Outrigger
Overland Outfitters
Page Boy Maternity
Panache Chocolatier
Parkway 600 Grill
Patricia Stevens Fashion
    Career College and
    Model Agency
Paul's Optical
Petite Style
Pierre Deux
Plaza Athletic Club
Plaza Hair Designs
Plaza Living Center
Plaza Merchants Association
Plaza News, Inc.
Plaza Pendleton
Plaza Shoe Shine
Plaza Tennis Courts
Plaza III Steakhouse
Plaza Weavers
Polo/Ralph Lauren

Popplewell & Co.
Price's Fine Chocolate
Pride of K.C. Carriages
The Raphael Hotel
Renner's Shoe Repair
Ritz-Carlton Hotel
Ruback's Fine Jewelry
Russell Stover Candies
Saffee's
Saks Fifth Ave.
Salon Klaus
Salon Pierre
Scandia Down Shop
Schaffer's Bridal Shop
Sculpture Gallery
Seville Cinema
Seville on the Plaza
Sharper Image
Shirtman
Shoe Express
St. Crispin Luggage and
    Leather Goods
The Sock Market
Starker's Restaurant
Steve's Shoes
Street Scene
Strauss-Peyton Photography
Superlatives
Swansons
Swirk Jewelry
T. J. Cinnamons Bakery
Talbots, Inc.
Taum Sauk Wilderness
    Outfitters
Timothy's
Tivol, Inc.
Topsy's Popcorn Shop
Trade Wind Wildlife Art
    Gallery
United Missouri Bank Plaza
Ups 'N Downs
Verl Custom Tailor
Vinca Ltd.
Voyages in Time
Ward Parkway Garage
White's Cards & Stationary
Williams-Sonoma, Inc.
Woolf Brothers

Halls, Swansons, and Saks Fifth Avenue typify the fashion-consciousness that draws millions of shoppers to the Plaza every year.

Swanson's

The comestibles at Crabtree & Evelyn (above) are as distinctive in their way as are (from left) the floral fabrics at Laura Ashley, the diamond baubles at Tivol Jewels, and the aromatic popcorn at Topsy's.

49

Jack Henry sales associate Willie Potts (above left) knows that Plaza patrons expect superior quality -- a value equally esteemed by (from left) Brooks Brothers, Abercrombie & Fitch, and Diebel's Sportsman's Gallery.

Plaza area employees Diane Schrupp and Jim Bowers browse through the many special interest publications at Plaza News.

Personalized stationery and engraving are just two of the custom services offered at Bennett Schneider Bookstore.

The Plaza isn't just for shopping. The many professional buildings located here offer a variety of services, from dentistry to watch repair. Dr. David P. Follmer, D.D.S., confers with patient Mary Barry.

Many Plaza area residents depend on Muehlbach's West, where the service-oriented traditions of the neighborhood grocery lives on. Produce manager Sean Meurrens assists Maebelle McCrorey in selecting fresh fruits.

SPECIAL
Kiwi Fruit
2 for 89¢

SPECIAL
Water Melon

SPECIAL
Limes
2 for 89

SPECIAL
Red Rome
Apples

SPECIAL
Large Grapefruit
89¢

SPECIAL
Lemons
4 for 1$

SPECIAL
Med. Or

The Christian Science Reading Room provides a quiet place to study for Doug and Abby Boudreaux. Reading room attendant Dolores Swender is happy to help.

Disc jockey Chuck McNasty projects his distinctive personality during a broadcast from KBEQ Radio Station.

Esoteric and one-of-a-kind delights for the palate can be found at The Better Cheddar (where Cheryl Williams prepares for a cheese tasting), and at Panache Chocolatier. Catch Kansas City owner Tina Pistilli offers not only tasty edibles but heartland memorabilia as well.

Old World
Epi Bread

56

The faithful customers of La Bonne Bouchée bakery insist that the shop's long loaves of crusty French bread and elegant pastries are the best this side of the Champs Élysées.

From aged Kansas City steaks at Plaza III, fresh seafood at the Bristol Bar & Grill, and delectable desserts at Fedora, to the venerable burger offerings at Winstead's, the Plaza's dining options are almost unlimited.

Providing a touch of New York's Central Park, horse-drawn carriages take Plaza visitors on a leisurely tour of the shopping district.

Easter and its well-attended parade prove nearly as popular as Christmastime on the Plaza.

Thousands of music lovers throng to the Brush Creek concerts in the Plaza where the air has been filled with the sounds of such artists as Ida McBeth, Count Basie, Jay McShann, Ray Charles, and Gary Burton

64

The festive character of the Plaza is abetted by the seasonal banners that festoon light posts throughout the shopping district

TA-DAAH!

SPRING ON
THE PLAZA

TA-DAAH!

SPRING ON
THE PLAZA

PLAZA IN
BLOOM

SEVIPLA
SPRING

PLAZA

PLAZA
ROYAL

PLAZA ART FAIR

2 HOUR
PARKING
7 AM-6 PM

66

The Plaza Art Fair

In 1932, the Plaza Merchants Association invited artists to show their works on an empty lot at the southwest corner of Nichols Road and Central. Almost ninety local artists leaned their pictures against trees or stood them up on the few benches placed around. People driving past on Nichols Road slowed down to see what it was all about.

This first fair didn't attract a steady stream of people, but many who came strolling by talked to the artists and looked at what they were exhibiting. Their paintings and drawings were priced from one to ten dollars. Because there were no lights, the fair was held only in the daylight hours.

The artists made a bit of money and many agreed that it was more important that they had had a good time and had developed a camaraderie with each other. Painting is a solitary endeavor and the fair offered artists a way to socialize together. The public got to know them, too. Friendships that lasted lifetimes were begun at that first fair.

The merchants felt it brought people to the Plaza so they decided to do it again the next year. Thus the Plaza Art Fair became an annual tradition anticipated each fall by both the public and the artists of the region. It is now recognized as one of the best art fairs in the country.

In the early years the fair was held at various locations. In the 1940s it was located just east of the Plaza Theatre where Chandler Court is now. Initially the artists built their own screens with chicken wire and prayed that wind or rain wouldn't ruin everything. In those days established artists such as Arthur Kraft (who sculpted the penguins in the courtyard at Nichols Road and Pennsylvania) and fifteen-year-old Jim Hamil might have had their booths side by side. (The first year that young Hamil exhibited, his paintings sold out the first night. Today he is one of Kansas City's most respected artists.

The fair has now grown to such size that Nichols Road from Wyandotte to Jefferson is blocked off and still some exhibitions overflow into several side streets. In 1988, there were 186 artists (mostly from outside the Kansas City area) showing oil paintings, watercolors, drawings, pottery, metalwork and woodcraft. The crowds have gotten so big that some complain that they have trouble seeing the works for the moving throng.

The fair was started to get people to come to the Plaza. It has accomplished that. It has also stimulated the creative talent of many artists and whetted the appetite of the art-buying public. Not a bad deal all around.

From its humble beginnings, the Plaza Art Fair has grown into a major regional showing of arts and crafts every September. Almost 200 artists display their work in the open-air booths.

For all that the Plaza offers in varied activities, its accommodation of the casual visitor in quiet pursuits is one of the district's most appealing characteristics.

The profusion of flowers and plants that add color to the Plaza throughout the year require the almost continuous attention of professional gardeners and plantsmen.

Plaza Sculpture

Though most visitors do not view the Plaza's sculpture with an academic eye (as is the class of students at left), many persons delight in a walking tour of this open-air "gallery." Herewith is a list of the major pieces of sculpture and their locations.

J.C. Nichols Memorial Fountain, sculpted by Henri Greber, Paris, 1910. J.C. Nichols Parkway, north of 47th Street.

Massasoit, sculpted by Cyrus Edwin Dallin and dedicated in 1979. J.C. Nichols Parkway, south of 47th Street.

Seville Light, with bronze chandelier towering 40 feet above water display. 47th street and J.C. Nichols Parkway.

Giralda Tower, Plaza's tallest tower with carillon bells sounding the hours daily. 47th Street and J.C. Nichols Parkway.

Boy and Hound, cast-lead piece from Bromsgrove Guild of Worcestershire, England. Ward Parkway and J.C. Nichols Parkway.

Study in Iron, iron gate designed by McArthur-Jarchow and fabricated by Oscar & Jerry Tooley, 1974. Wyandotte and ward Parkway.

Madonna and Child, Carrara marble reproduction of Michelangelo's masterpiece. On 47th Street, between Wyandotte and J.C. Nichols Parkway.

Fountain of Bacchus, 1911 lead statuary from the Bromsgrove Guild of Worcestershire, England. Wyandotte and 47th Street.

Ruth, original Carrara marble by Pasquale Romanelli of Florence, Italy. Wyandotte and Nichols Road.

Italian Wellhead, ornate wrought iron wellhead, circa 1750. Artist unknown. 47th Street and Wyandotte.

Neptune Fountain, Greek god of the sea with trident, dolphin and horse. Wornall Road and 47th Street.

Panorama of the Americas, 1964 porcelain mural by Kansas City artist John Podrebarac. Wornall Road and 47th Street.

Bronze Boar Fountain, reproduction of 1857 bronze by the Italian artist Benelli. On 47th Street, between Broadway and Central.

Spanish Bullfight Mural, hand-crafted ceramic mural from Seville, Spain. On Central, between Nichols Road and 47th Street.

Boy and Frog Fountain, original bronze and marble fountain by Raffaello Romanelli of Florence, Italy. Nichols Road and Central.

Allen Memorial Fountain, bronze and marble memorial to the daughter and son-in-law of J.C. Nichols, carved by S. Gemignani. Nichols Road, between Broadway and Central.

Pool of Four Fauns, depicts four children of the Roman spirit Faunus. Nichols Road and Broadway.

Mermaid Pool, inlaid ceramic tile pool adorned with Carrara mermaids. Nichols Road and Broadway.

Pomona, original bronze of the Roman goddess of vineyards and orchards by Italian sculptor Donatello Gabrielli. Ward Parkway and Broadway.

Boy with the Thorn, replica of Florentine original dating to fifth century B.C. Ward Parkway and Wornall Road.

Diana, Roman goddess of the moon, sculpted by Bernhard Zuckermann, 1912. Ward Parkway and Wornall Road.

The Wagon Master, an L.E. "Gus" Shafer original bronze tribute to Santa Fe Trail travelers. Ward Parkway, west of Wornall Road.

Married Love, Oscar Nemon's bronze rendering of Sir Winston and Lady Churchill, dedicated in 1984. Wornall Road and Ward Parkway.

The Orange Court of Seville, Spain, a Spanish orange grove depicted in 64 quarry tiles by Kansas City artist Carolyn Payne. Broadway, between Ward Parkway and Nichols Road.

April, bronze of a young girl watering spring flowers by Santa Fe artist Glenna Goodacre, Pennsylvania, between Ward Parkway and Nichols Road.

The Invincible Spirit, bronze of American bald eagle and two nesting eaglets by Oregon naturalist-sculptor Lorenzo E. Ghiglieri. Broadway and Nichols Road.

Windfall, 1987 bronze by Chapel depicts a blue heron with fallen limbs and brush over a mountain stream. Ward Parkway and Pennsylvania.

Children at Play, marble wall fountain from an original model by Cipriani. Broadway, between Nichols Road and 47th Street.

Time Tower, majestic clock housed within Spanish-inspired structure overlooking Brush Creek. Ward Parkway, between Broadway and Pennsylvania.

Pegasus, a Wheeler Williams bronze of the mythological winged horse. 47th Street, east of Broadway.

Quiet Talk, 1987 bronze by Utah sculptor Dennis Smith. Broadway and 47th Street.

The Last Supper, a nearly life-size basswood carving of da Vinci's masterpiece by Domenic Zappia. Unity Church, 707 W. 47th Street.

Sleeping Child, and original in Carrara marble by Ferdinande Andreini, 1963. 47th Street, west of Broadway.

Out to Lunch, life-sized bronze by J. Seward Johnson, 1977. Nichols Road, between Pennsylvania and Jefferson.

Diana, life-sized bronze by Richard McDermott Miller. Nichols Road and Jefferson.

Court of the Penguins, trio of five-foot bronzes reproduced from original miniatures by Kansas City artist Arthur Kraft. Nichols Road, between Pennsylvania and Jefferson.

Untitled, abstract bronze of arms embracing waters of fountain-sculpture designed by Kansas City architect Robert Berkebile and sculptor Norman Brunelli, 1971. Jefferson and Ward Parkway.

The "Sleeping Child" is a perennial favorite of sculpture viewers on the Plaza. A thoughtful Plaza citizen sometimes protects the statue with a blanket on cold, snowy winter nights.

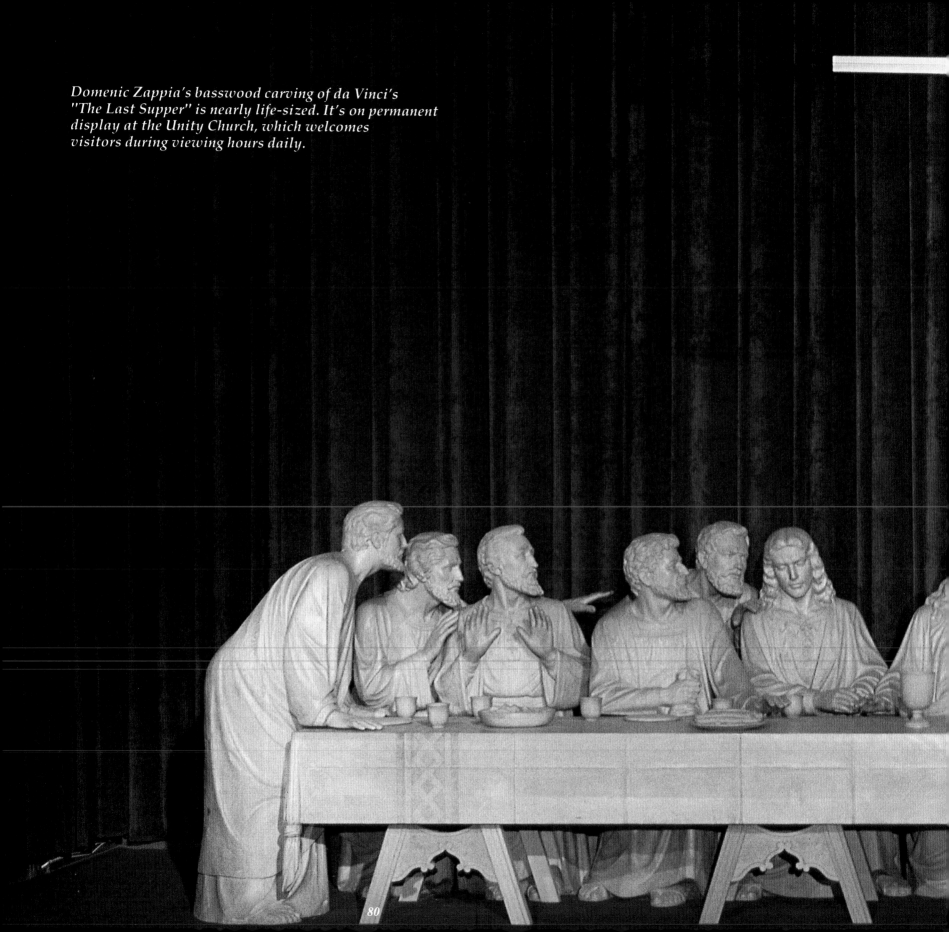

Domenic Zappia's basswood carving of da Vinci's
"The Last Supper" is nearly life-sized. It's on permanent
display at the Unity Church, which welcomes
visitors during viewing hours daily.

Streams of water become part of the action at several sculptural fountains on the Plaza--as evidenced by these figures.

Figures of Pegasus, children talking and Bacchus indicate a diverse thematic span in the Plaza's sculptural panoply.

"QUIET TALK"

83

The Carrara marble statue of Ruth is just one of many figures that constitute the city's biggest outdoor "art gallery." Other popular works include (from left) Chief Massasoit, the Wagonmaster, Winston and Clementine Churchill, Ruth (detail), Boy with Eel, and the Fauns.

The Court of the Penguins provides a quiet respite from the bustling Plaza streets. A trio of five-foot bronze penguins are reproductions of the original miniatures created by Kansas City artist Arthur Kraft in 1979.

timothy's

The Seville Light provides a welcoming beacon to visitors entering the Plaza. The light rises from a collection pool, with a bronze chandelier towering nearly 40 feet above the water.

Held by many to be one of the Plaza's most graceful fountains, the water design at Woolf Brothers is topped by a figure of Pomona.

The J.C. Nichols Memorial Fountain at 47th Street and J.C. Nichols Parkway is a tribute to the founder of the Plaza. The fountain's four horsemen were sculpted in Paris in 1910 by Henri Greber.

Carillon bells sound the hours daily from Giralda, the Plaza's tallest tower. It was created in 1967 by Bernhard Zuckermann of Carrara, Italy.

95

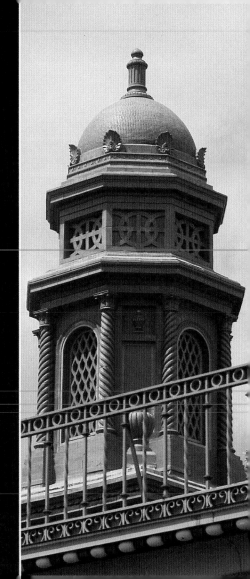

The spectacular fountain of Diana incorporates one of the largest man-made waterfalls in America. Sculpted by Bernhard Zuckermann, the piece depicts the Roman goddess of the moon with her three cherubs.

One of Kansas City's most popular hotels, the
Ritz-Carlton reflects elegance inside and out.

Built as the Alameda Plaza, the hotel is now the Ritz-Carlton and offers an ambience of luxury, beauty and service.

A winter snowfall heightens the enchantment of the Plaza lights.

Lights

In 1925, Charles Pitrat, head of the Nichols Company maintenance operation, placed a single six-foot strand of sixteen colored light bulbs across the doorway of the Suydam building, the Plaza's first building. Who would have thought that this modest holiday gesture would start a Christmas tradition that would gain worldwide attention?

People have been fascinated by these lights ever since. The lighting ceremony draws bigger crowds each year. On Thanksgiving night, 1988, 275,000 people filled Plaza streets to witness the lighting ceremony. In nearby hotel rooms (reserved a year in advance) more watched from above to get the over-all effect of the lights.

It took 156,000 light bulbs to illuminate the Plaza for the 1988 season. The tradition grew just the way the Plaza did. As buildings were added so were lights. When the Plaza Theatre was completed in 1928, Pitrat strung lights across 47th Street to reach the theater building. The next year he outlined the buildings and towers with lights. And so it went, adding more lights to frame more buildings. Putting up those first lights took one man and a ladder. The chore is definitely more difficult today. A special crew handles the forty-six miles of wiring necessary to carry the current to the bulbs. After the first of the year the crew starts taking the lights down from the buildings and carefully marks the wires according to building and position. The crew has all spring and summer to check fuse boxes, circuits and wiring and to replace all the bulbs. Special waterproof sockets are used. All new light bulbs are used every year to insure that they will last through the holiday season.

The lights are installed in the fall using ladders, boom trucks and a specially constructed chair like the boatswain's chair used aboard ships. To ascend those tile-glazed domes and towers, workmen use ropes and shoes similar to those used in mountain climbing, to keep their footing.

As Thanksgiving approaches, light rehearsals are held in the dead of night to guarantee that all the lights come on at the same time. Once the switch is pulled at the lighting ceremony, a timer turns the lights on every night at dusk and off at about 1:30 a.m. Even after Thanksgiving workmen are kept busy, usually replacing as many as 5,000 bulbs that, for some reason, go out.

Many feel the holidays wouldn't be the same without a trip to see the Plaza lights. They never fail to bring out childlike wonderment in both young and old.

During the holiday season, Kansas City drivers deliberately route themselves through the Plaza to view the shopping district's annual display of Christmas lights.

The Plaza's many towers become fanciful structures when outlined in thousands of colored lights.

Hundreds of colored tiles inset in structures throughout the
Plaza touch on a wide variety of subjects and themes.

Bas relief terra cotta ornamentation,
found throughout the Plaza, enhances
the Spanish-style architecture.

119

The Nelson-Atkins Museum of Art is host to the largest collection of Henry Moore bronzes outside the sculptor's native England. The gallery in 1989 created a special outdoor garden-gallery to display the pieces.

Loose Park, on Wornall Road just south of the Plaza, offers a blooming season of botanical splendor that draws visitors from the nearby shopping district.

In 1978, Christo, the internationally known environmental sculptor, wrapped the sidewalks of Loose Park in saffron-colored cloth. Few Kansas Citians were without an opinion about the artistic merits of the end result.

It is understandable why joggers prefer the paths of Loose Park. In the morning mists or at dusk, runners can be observed throughout the beautiful grounds.

Kansas City sculptor Dale Eldred's sculpture, "Brush Creek Solar Field,"
included five hundred light-refracting pylons that changed color
with the movement of the sun. Eldred chairs the sculpture
department at the nearby Kansas City Art Institute.

126

In the winter, the Plaza is the scene of the ice sculpting competition sponsored by the National Chef's Association.

Frank Lloyd Wright, legend of American architecture, in 1940 designed the Community Christian Church on Main Street near 47th street.

Buyers and sellers haggle over prices on the floor of the Kansas City Board of Trade. Founded in 1856, it is the largest market in the world for trading hard red winter wheat.

The decorative milepost on the north bank of
Brush Creek indicates mileages between Kansas City
and its sister cities around the world.

Sister Cities
of
Kansas City
Missouri

Seville, Spain
← 4700 miles.
Freetown, Sierra
Leone, Africa
← 5000 miles.

Acknowledgements

Harrow Books wishes to thank the J.C. Nichols Company, the Plaza Merchants Association, the individual shop owners and managers of the Country Club Plaza and others who cooperated in the gathering of the material for this book.

The editor gratefully acknowledges the loan of historical photographs from:

The Kansas City Public Library, Missouri Valley Room

The Plaza Library

The Johnson County Library

The J.C. Nichols Company Archive

Joint Collection, Western Missouri Historical Manuscript Collection and the State Historical Society of Missouri Manuscripts at the University of Missouri-Kansas City

Wilborn & Associates

Printed in the United States
SUN GRAPHICS, INCORPORATED
Parsons, Kansas